ONCE UPON AN ISLAND

ONCE UPON AN ISLAND

IMAGES OF VANCOUVER ISLAND

MICHAEL ORTON

Orca Book Publishers

Canadian Cataloguing in Publication Data
Orton, Michael, 1947–
     Once upon an island

ISBN 0-920501-82-6

1. Vancouver Island (B.C.) — Pictorial works.
I. Title.
FC3844.4.O77 1992   971.1'2'00222   C92-091497-7
F1089 V3O77 1992

Publication assistance provided by The Canada Council
Design by Susan Fergusson
Printed and bound in Hong Kong

Orca Book Publishers
PO Box 5626, Station B
Victoria, BC Canada
V8R 5S4

To my many island friends, I hope you enjoy this vision of "home" and continue to explore and appreciate this marvellous place.

To my parents, Joan and Ken, for their constant encouragement; sons, Jeremy and Ryan, for understanding my dream, and especially to my wife Mary, for without her love and inspiration this book would not exist.

INTRODUCTION

Photography for me is an intimate journey of discovery and exploration, and, if on the voyage I am lucky enough to be moved by the landscape, then I consider the ensuing images successful. *Once Upon an Island* is a collection of these moments. I feel fortunate indeed to have been able to experience and record them on film, and, though it is unlikely these opportunities will ever be repeated, I am constantly fuelled with the knowledge that there are new, previously unimagined places on this island and elsewhere to be explored and treasured.

The Journey Begins

Dawn

The birth of dawn and the accompanying spectacle of light is a powerfully motivating force for me. As I stood on a hillside this frosted winter morning unfolded into a tapestry of crimson. I felt an eerie sensation of being enveloped by the sky itself as it swept from horizon to horizon — the ultimate awakening.

The long drive through darkness and dense fog was suddenly rewarded. A single eagle presses into the now magenta sky, leaving his roost in a tall fir, jagged against the soft clouds behind. An effortless pulse of wings, then he glides silently across the soft grey blanket to a distant perch. I photograph quietly, carefully, doing nothing to disturb the reverence of dawn.

Winter Morn

Fisherman

Although I am not a fisherman, a scene like this explains why so many can't wait to get out on the water.

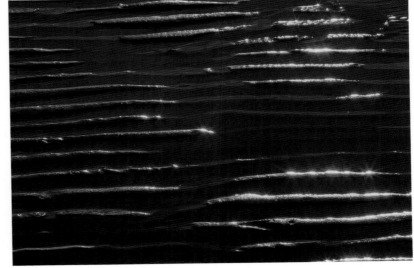

A treasure left by the retreating tide. I have only moments to capture the gold before it turns to sand.

Real Gold

Misty Morning

Facing page

Passing by

My experiences of seeing the world through a camera's lens have deepened my respect for the natural world. I can no more change the time of sunrise than I can turn the tides or hold back a cloud front. This spot where I stand to photograph at daybreak will be under eight feet of water by noon, these ominous claws of stone lurking beneath the waves to smash any boat passing too close.

I never tire of driving the backroads of Vancouver Island. On this day the still radiant autumn sun slowly dissolved the early morning mist on Sproat Lake.

Backroads

Cathedral

Shafts of light wedged through elegant firs create an ethereal atmosphere over a split-rail fence.

Misted Meadow

Sailboat anchored at dawn

When the waters are warm and the air near freezing, small lakes and rivers are crowned with an aura of rising mist. This morning I stalk the river bank, careful not to alarm a line of ducks, though they seem more concerned with the commotion upstream in the rapids where gulls have converged on the shallows to gorge on spawned-out salmon.

Light

Each sunrise is unique, as the seasons and skies change, and the mood evoked by each varies. Dawn light never fails to give me a feeling of rejuvenation.

*Road's
End*

After threading its way thousands of miles across the vastness of the country, the Trans Canada Highway comes to an abrupt end on a pier in Tofino. Most mornings swirling Pacific mists play a game of hide-and-seek with the distant islands.

Facing page

Walking on water

Compared to others, the island that we live on is of considerable size.
It is, however, still an island, and that is never more evident than
when I stand on the shore and watch the ferry sailing away.

Islands

The Water's Edge

E ven the smallest stream, like each
one of us, must find its own path
through the heart of the woods.

The Stream

West Coast

On the island's western edge the Pacific Ocean rules. In a cold mist we crawl and climb through a gnarled tangle of driftwood, wind-blown pine and salal to witness the rhythmic attack of icy waves on the rocky shoreline.

Languid pools, like enormous mirrors, cause me to hold my breath so as not to disturb the perfect surface.

Suspended

Millstream River,
Bowen Park,
Nanaimo

On a sunny afternoon off Victoria a fleet of sailboats and a cluster of soft clouds meet on the horizon.

New life

Resilient and determined seem inadequate descriptions of this tiny fellow. In two feet of water, and twenty feet from shore he struggles for his place in the natural world.

I would just as soon not know how nature works marvels such as this. I am content to know that, for those who want to discover this world, these works of magic are there to be found.

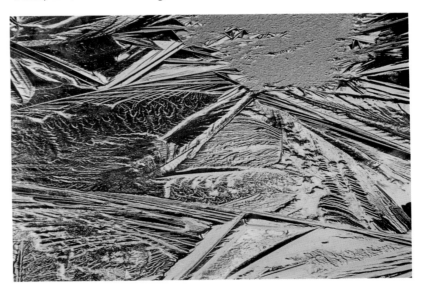

Following page

The tides, though often merciless in their pounding of the coast, also nourish this healthy colony of shellfish.

Schooner Beach

The rugged west coast at its most serene.

Previous page

Tugboat

Rolling silently off the Pacific, a blanket of fog envelopes what was moments earlier a sun-basked beach, leaving this pair of gulls unsure of their next move.

Just a visitor

Evening Light

The palette

Goldstream Park

Dancing off the face of the cliff, the cascade tumbles down to become a quiet pool once again.

The Magic of Spring

S pring in Beacon Hill Park is a fairyland as trees thick with blossom cloud the air with fragrance and colour. Delicate pink petals carpet the pathways and float feather-like on the still surface of the ponds.

A friend's field of flowers

Spring woods in the rain

Each spring I head for the marshes where one particular plant grows with exuberance. The show begins with a bright yellow hood piercing the muddy earth, followed by lush green leaves unfolding in an elegant display. With their upright rigidity, I can't help but think how much they resemble soldiers at attention.

The texture and tones of a stone ledge frame the outstretched leaves of a Dwarf Dogwood.

Not far from the island's main highway, and often shielded from view by a wall of trees, are many peaceful pockets of farmland.

Scouring Rush

How could such a pristine emerald creation earn the label "scouring"? Perhaps as the seasons change, so will the plant. For now I marvel at the translucent, vibrant quality of the stems.

Facing page

Tulips in a Spring Rain

On the grounds of a retired sea captain's estate I stumble upon a cornucopia of mature trees. The dozens of species planted and nurtured long ago have been left on their own for years. The orchard still blossoms in the spring, though little fruit will show in the fall. Untouched by the pruner's sheers, they grow and flow together.

Walking the banks of the river near my home has rewarded me with many visual delights. The winter runoff has subsided and the gentle green waters blend with vibrant new growth on the shore.

The River's Path

Facing page

Even with this challenging environment, succulents, lichen, and hardy grasses burst with lush green growth in the cool spring rains. Marvellously adapted, they provide a patchwork of colour to rocky outcroppings only a few feet from the saltwater swells.

From within a cave a family of finger-ferns stretch for the warm sunlight.

One of the greatest pleasures I have as a photographer is the study of flowers. The myriad of designs and purity of colour are constant sources of wonder and amazement. These stately spires with their subtle colour variations were mine to explore for the duration of the evening light.

Blue-eyed Mary in the spring

Gifts

A tree can give many things.
In the fall it can yield baskets
of fruit, and in the summer a
cool umbrella of shade, but in the
spring a tree gives pure joy.

The Paintbox of Butchart Gardens

While thousands of others shuffle down stone pathways and pose in tight clusters for their "we were there" pictures, I unfold a garbage bag and sit down on the ground in the midst of a sea of colour. "Hey, Edith, look at this guy down here. He's got a telephoto lens and it's right in the flower bed." But already I am lost in the profusion of bloom and colour, and the voices fade.

An Island Home

A simple footpath meanders around and across this lovely island park — through arbutus, garry oak, fir, cedar and maple. A favourite place in spring and fall.

Newcastle Island

Years ago parts of the island yielded a rich harvest of black gold in the form of coal. In spite of the dangers, miners descended into the bowels of the earth to extract the precious bounty. To them it represented life itself. Now, as I stand where once a miners' town thrived, I imagine the horses and carts drawing loads of coal along muddy pathways. I see the soiled faces of the men; in the distance the clatter of machines and the hiss of steam rattle the otherwise silent surrounding forest.

Coalmine Area,
Nanaimo

I set out one afternoon during a summer rain. As I drove by a meadow I had passed numerous times, the heavy, black clouds opened just enough to let the sun pass through. Suddenly the landscape was transformed. At first I was awestruck, unable to do anything but gaze at the amazing light. There was time for but three photographs and then it was gone. When I spotted that magic glow further up the road, I raced to catch up. I only had time to steal this rainbow before the surging clouds again devoured the sun. Moments later a torrent of raindrops tattooed the windshield, washing the landscape clean.

Rainbow

Cathedral Grove,
Sacred Home of Forest Giants

Autumn light possesses a special quality, one which often kindles a mood of nostalgia. I remember as a boy playing on a swing just like this one. Recollections of tree houses, special hiding places, and secret passwords whispered gave this moment sentimental meaning.

Daydream

Kayaker,
Cox Bay,
West Coast

A summer's eve is almost over, and, though this kayaker had been in the ocean for what seemed like hours, he would continue until darkness fell. The look of satisfaction on his wet, smiling face affirmed his love of this place, where there is always one more wave to ride.

Hydrangea Blue

My friend

I have photographed horses on many occasions and have almost always found them to be willing and cooperative subjects. I talked slowly while assembling my camera and tripod as quickly as possible and this fellow seemed to understand. He remained motionless, allowing me to compose and shoot; then he sauntered over to the fence for a visit.

Snowfall on the island, though an infrequent occurrence, often has a storybook quality to it. Not usually driven by the wind, it arrives silently and often unexpected. On these occasions I traverse the backroads of a winter wonderland, drinking in the scenes, hoping it will last for at least a few days.

One Misty Morning

Later That Same Morning

Clouds at Play

Fishing and photography are in some ways quite similar. I am sure that many of those who fish are just as happy to feel the sun on their faces, the skip of the fly on the river's ripple and the pulse of the current against their legs as they are to actually catch a fish. Likewise, I spend many hours in the outdoors and never use my camera at all. Today, however, my catch is the fisherman!

Rainforest

A timber trestle descends into the rainforest on the west coast, and in a few moments one enters a place of almost tropical magic. Eerie mosses festoon tree limbs, glistening green leaves of immense proportions umbrella the forest floor where airy ferns radiate upwards in graceful arches. Surrounded by such luxurious growth, tranquillity is inevitable.

Facing page

The lighthouse on Quadra Island stands guard over a driftwood playhouse.

Changing Seasons

Autumn

Facing page

The different seasons,
with their variations in
light and colour, provide
many opportunities to
re-interpret familiar scenes.

Harvest
Forgotten

Winter's short, cold days grasp the landscape, and in the early hours a freezing mist disguises familiar scenes with its monochrome mask. The sweet scent of autumn has faded. An apple tree, only weeks ago laden with fruit, stands abandoned.

Paradise
Meadows

I remember being able to hear my heartbeat in the
cool silence of evening as we waited for the last light
to capture the soft undulations of this scene.

On a secluded lake near Mt. Cosmos two fishermen spend a fall day drifting with the breeze.

Facing page

I stepped hesitantly along a roadside fence on this crisp winter morning, regretting each footstep, for all around were fallen leaves, each one a frosted work of art.

After an area is logged, unwanted deciduous trees proliferate on the hillsides. On this misty fall morning on a trail above Sproat Lake I stop to admire the sweep of seasonal colour they have offered.

Indian Summer

In a darkened wood maple leaves reach randomly for light.

For those fortunate enough to have an old apple tree grace their yard, autumn is a splendid time to sit beneath the transformed canopy of leaves.

The mystically monochromatic stillness of Sproat Lake forms a soft backdrop to autumn's last surge of life.

Strathcona Park,
Alpine Area

Walking in the Woods

November 29th

I always ask myself how an image makes me feel. With these stark, barren branches scratching at a sombre sky, and a cold rain falling, the answer here was "chilled, emotionally and physically." Shapes and faces grew unbidden from the snarl of naked limbs. On the horizon a line of haunting figures paused on their march to the crest.

Winter Waterland

Day's End

Westcoast Moonscape

The still night air carries the faint whisper of the distant waves. The grove of dead cedars with their carved trunks and maimed limbs frame a thin moon as bats flit and swerve over my head. I feel uneasy, alone and exposed as the last light fades, a long way from home and safety.

Buttertubs Marsh, Irises and Rushes

Friends

The joy in the youngster's voices bounced as beautifully as the evening light.

Their laughter fades. The drying pools in a sheltered cove reflect the evening's last light as sandpipers scurry to probe the wet sand, knowing the tide will soon cover their feeding ground again.

Visitors explore the pools left by the receding tide.

Waiting Freighter

I enjoy watching the steady procession of ocean-going ships that pass through the Strait. A freighter lies anchored offshore, and though these ships are enormous, the expanse of water and coastal mountains dwarf them.

*Westwood Lake
Nightfall*

Facing page

This cool, autumn evening I have donned my high-top boots to investigate the graceful grasses and reeds at the edge of a pond. I move slowly in the rising mist, carefully skirting the water's edge, never quite comfortable, for there is nothing like a plunge to the waist in ice-cold water to shorten a field trip.

The distant crack of a beaver's tail splits the still evening air. All but the fearless swallows give up the airspace to the bats who begin to feed over the water. The blackened woods behind creak and snap, stirring my imagination in unwanted directions. A mile-long walk through the darkness awaits.

Westcoast Eve

In unerring repetition the tide returns, nibbling and sloshing over rippled sandbars, calmly engulfing all in its path. It is time to cross the spit and return to the cabin to be lulled to sleep by the gentle voice of Pacific swells.

A Sunset Walk

Facing Page

I marvel at the effect of even
the smallest waves on the shoreline. They scramble and shuffle
small stones, polishing them to
near-perfect roundness. When
the stone is too large to turn,
a sculpture is created.

Standing in the Sky, Tofino

The sweep of a wave and a wash of evening light transform a beach into a river of gold.

Waves of thunder rolled across the distant sky on this warm
August night. As they grew nearer, a crowd of curious island-
ers gathered on the beach. We sat on driftwood logs, gazing
up, curiously quiet, anticipating. And we were not to be disap-
pointed. The sky opened and the spectacle began.

Photographing the Island: Technical Notes

I couldn't begin to document all of the photographic possibilities that present themselves to the avid photographer on this lovely island of ours. However, here are some general notes on equipment, locations and technique that work for me and that I hope will assist other photographers.

My equipment is very lightweight and simple, yet it offers me the exposure and composition flexibility that I require. Here it is: a substantial Manfrotto tripod which I use constantly, a pair of Pentax ME Super 35mm bodies with 24mm, 28mm, 50mm, 70-210mm (and sometimes a 60-300mm) lenses accompany me on my journeys. I used only skylight and polarizing filters for the photographs in this book, although I now have a few other subtle filters (pale blue and pale amber). My film of choice is Fujichrome 50 and 100.

Seasons

I prefer the spring and fall because of the subtle and varying light and weather conditions. The soft rains of spring or overcast days are ideal for exploring the woods with such mystical trees as arbutus, moss-covered maples and twisted garry oak. Amongst the large cedar and fir there are often sweeping mists which render truly magical photographs. A tripod is necessary under these low light conditions, and even though there is no direct sunlight, a polarizing filter will remove reflections from leaves, producing vibrant, lush greens. Flowers both wild and domestic abound on the island and once again the overcast light in the spring renders beautifully saturated colours. My favourite lens in this situation is a 70-210mm at f4 and careful selective focusing at or near ground level.

The fall offers warm days and cool nights, and these in turn cause mist to rise from lakes and to settle in valleys and meadows. The morning sun dissipates this moisture quickly, so I will often set out before dawn to arrive at my destination. A simple rule for exposure is: to keep a light misted scene light, add light (overexpose slightly), and to keep a dark scene dark, such as a silhouette, take light away (underexpose).

Locations

The east shorelines of Vancouver Island are mostly sheltered and offer everything from sandy to stony beaches, rock cliffs and interesting cove and harbour formations. Reflections on tidal pools and sandbars, and those of colourful boats are common subjects, with sunrise over Georgia Strait my favourite time of day almost anywhere along this coast. A quick check of the tide tables in the newspaper tells me whether to expect a sandy beach or several feet of water at any given time.

Rural areas with small farms are also scattered along the eastern side of the island and I will often travel these backroads in the spring and fall. Horses, isolated meadows and rustic cedar fences and barns are common along with roadside flowers.

The west coast of the island means the Pacific Ocean — awesome waves, wind-swept trees and cliffs, rainforest and sunsets. Evening summer light here is beautiful and the occasional summer fog off the ocean will produce some unique photo possibilities. All lenses, from a 24mm for capturing vast seascapes to a 300mm to isolate a fishboat bobbing in the swells, can be used here, making this area a favourite for photography workshops.

A Note about Technique

The soft focus images in this book are in fact two photographs. One is a controlled amount out of focus and overexposed one stop; the second is in sharp focus and overexposed two stops. I then sandwich the two transparencies to produce the final image. This gives a mystical, romantic feel to the resulting photograph. It does, however, require a certain amount of visual discipline as it involves zooming and focusing simultaneously in order to have both the colour slide and the detail slide combine to produce one image. Once again a job for Mr. Tripod.

A Final Note

What is photography all about? Well, for me it means seeing in the purest sense — exploring and discovering. So if you bring your camera, use a little vision, a dash of imagination and a bit of perseverance, you will be well rewarded here on Vancouver Island.

Michael Orton